Introduction To Offender Profiling

Analysing the Criminal Mind

History, Currently Usage, Strengths and Weaknesses

Teresa Clyne, B.A. (Hons.), MSc

Author: Teresa Clyne BA, MSc

Teresa is currently a Lecturer in Law and Forensic Psychology. Her research encompasses an array of diverse areas, which amongst other things, includes; Restorative Justice, geographical profiling, geo-spatial behaviour of serial killers, offender profiling, the legal system; Gardai and police interviewing; internet sex offending; mental maps of computer criminals and risk assessment work.

© 2016 Teresa Clyne

The author, publisher and distributor of this book have made every effort to ensure the accuracy, completeness and reliability of the content of this publication. In all instances you should take advice in relation to any local policies or procedures prior to making any decisions or taking any actions relating to the subject matter contained herein.

No warranty is given or implied with respect to its content. Consequently in no event will the author, publisher or distributor be liable for direct, indirect, special, incidental or consequential damages arising out of the use of the information contained in this book.

All information used in this introductory textbook is intended for information purposes only and does not represent any type of advice. The information in this introductory textbook has not been written to meet any individual requirements and no reader should act or refrain from acting on such information without first verifying the information and as necessary obtaining professional advice. Teresa Clyne expressly disclaims all liability for any direct, indirect or consequential loss or damage occasioned from the use or inability to use this textbook whether directly or indirectly resulting from inaccuracies, defects, errors, whether typographical or otherwise, omissions, out of date information or otherwise, even if such loss was reasonably foreseeable. While all care is taken to ensure that all works used is cited Teresa Clyne accepts no responsibility for any omissions, should any of your work be used and not cited please do contact the author at teresaclyne@mail.com and it will be rectified immediately.

Contents

Introduction to Offender Profiling vi
   Analysing the Criminal Mind vi

Chapter 1 – What is Offender Profiling? 1
   Media Portrayal 1
   What is it? 3
      Criminal Profiling: 4
      History of Criminal Profiling 5
      The differences between forensic psychology and profiling. 6
      What makes a serial offender? 7
      Mental illness and serial offending 9
      Psychopathy and serial offending 11
      Typologies of killers 15
      Predatory Agression 16
      Techniques used in criminal profiling. 19
      Stages in profiling 19
      Paraphilias 21
      Psychoanalysis in criminal profiling 24
      The traits of an organised killer 27
      Organized crime scene suggests an offender: 29
      The traits of a disorganised killer 30
      Disorganized crime scene suggests an offender: 31

Chapter 2– Background and History of Offender Profiling 32

Chapter 3 – History of Use of Offender Profiling 35

Jack the Ripper 36

The Babes of Inglewood 38

Adolf Hitler and the OSS 41

The Mad Bomber 43

The Yorkshire Ripper 46

Offender Profiling in the U.S. – The FBI's Behavioral Analysis Unit 48

Offender Profiling in the UK/Ireland, ... 50

    David Canter and Identifying the Railway Ripper 50

An Old Idea Finally Comes to Fruition 52

Chapter 4 – Offender Profiling Today 53

    Overview –How is it Used Today? 53

    Geographical Profiling 54

    Guiding the Investigation 58

    Crime Linkage 60

    Categorization 62

Chapter 5 – Serial killers, spree killers, mass killers 64

    Family annihilations are Mass murder 68

    Serial killers can be defined as; 70

    The top 10 characteristics of a serial killer 98

        1.   Cruelty to animals 100

        2.   Abused as children 100

        3.   Wet the bed 100

        4.   Narcissistic 100

        5.   Pyromania 101

6.	Impotent	101
7.	Developing voyeurism and fetishism in adulthood	101
8.	Brain Trauma	102
9.	Dysfunctional families	74
10.	Alcohol and drug abuse	74

Ireland's Serial Killers 75

Chapter 6 – Strengths and Weaknesses of Profiling 108

Strengths 108
Geographical Profiling 108
Winnowing 111

Concerns and Weaknesses 113
Lack of Empirical Evidence 113
What is Success? 116
Admissibility and Use in Courtroom 119

Chapter 6 – Other Applications and Conclusions 121
Other Applications 121
Conclusions 124

Bibliography 125

Introduction to Offender Profiling

Analysing the Criminal Mind

This guide provides clear and concise information on central issues such as the origins of criminal profiling from the American Top Down Theories of Offenders behaviours and actions to the UKs Bottom Up Theories, it has its roots in FBI profiling methodology and limitations of profiling are also explained to the reader.

If you are interested in criminal profiling and would like to learn more, An Introduction to Offender Profiling; analysing the Criminal Mind is the perfect place to start.

Have you ever wondered how profilers profile offenders?, how they can gather so much information about a suspect from such things as the age and race and gender of the offender from the crime scene or victims.

Offender Profiling providing a likely description of an offender based on an analysis of

– Crime scene
– The victim
– Other available evidence

Offender profiling does not solve crime or identify individuals, but it does provide a means of narrowing the range of potential suspects (Holmes & Holmes 1996)

The British method – a 'bottom-up' approach to Offender Profiling

Research from "Canter" reveals that the bottom up approach is:

Based on psychological theories and methodologies (cognitive social)

Formulated to show how and why variations in criminal behaviour occur

Consistent within actions of offenders

More objective & reliable than the American Top down model. Canter (1980s)

Approaches to profiling – Top Down – The American method

Classification system for several serious crimes, especially rape and murder

For example: murders classified as 'organised' or 'disorganised'

Organised offenders Features:

Planned crimes

Self-control

Covers tracks

Victim is stranger

Characteristics:

Intelligent

Skilled occupation

Socially competent

Angry/depressed

Disorganised Offenders Features:

Unplanned crimes

Haphazard

Leaves clues

Characteristics:

Socially inadequate

Unskilled

First/last born child

Lives alone

Knows victim

Confused/frightened.   (Rossiter et al 1988)

Introduction to Offender Profiling

Chapter 1 – What is Offender Profiling?

Offender profiling otherwise known as criminal profiling.

Before we delve deeply into the subject of Offender Profiling, it helps to get an understanding of what we are talking about. Most people have heard the terns Offender Profiling or Criminal Profiling used in the media and therefore have certain assumptions and understandings that come to mind when those terms come up. Some of those assumptions are accurate, and others are based on inaccurate media portrayal and are inaccurate. In this Chapter we will address what Offender Profiling is and what does and does not do. Please note that the terms Offender Profiling and Criminal Profiling are often used interchangeably, but we will use the term Offender Profiling here.

Media Portrayal

There are two main ways that we tend to see Offender Profiling handled in the media. Probably the one that jumps to mind for most people is the fictional context.

There have been several television shows where the hero (or heroine) assists authorities in examining a crime by taking a look at the evidence, and seeing some small clue or clues that no one else thought was important, determines various details about the perpetrator. Usually, the hero is aware of some unusual knowledge or trivia that allows only that person to use the clues in question to lead to the arrest of the perpetrator, typically moments before the

Introduction to Offender Profiling

perpetrator strikes again. There are various television shows and movies that use this sort of a pattern and the hero/heroine who provides the offender profile may be anything from a writer, a crime scene investigator or a medical doctor. This type of a story line has recently been popular in movies and television, but in written media dates back to at least the 1800's when Sherlock Holmes explained such a discovery to Mr. Watson as "Elementary." (Doyle, 1894)

The other context in which Offender Profiling frequently appears in media is in news reports. Often we hear discussions of Offender Profiling with relation to things like airport security. A Google search of the phrase "offender profiling terrorism" returns over 390,000 results. Sometimes this is in the context of whether or not offender profiling is helpful or not in relation to terrorism. Sometimes the discussion is related to news events and the relationship between Racial Profiling and Offender Profiling.

Introduction to Offender Profiling

What is it?

Despite the fact that fictional media has been portraying Offender Profiling for a long time, there is no standard definition of the term that all practitioners of Offender Profiling use. The Oxford Dictionary defines the term, which was first used in the 1980's, as follows:

> Offender Profiling: A system of analysing and recording the probable psychological and behavioural characteristics of the unknown perpetrators of specific crimes so they can be matched with the known habits and personalities of suspects. (The Oxford University Press, 2016).

Other terms and phrases are used to mean the same thing, such as criminal profiling and criminal behaviour profiling, or simply behaviour profiling. These terms mean basically the same thing, and are often used interchangeably in the criminal investigation context. The FBI's Law Enforcement Bulletin has stated that the lack of a universal definition "lies at the heart of many contentions." (J. Amber Scherer, 2014).

There are a few things that Offender Profiling is not and does not do, and understanding those is helpful in understanding what Offender Profiling actually is and how it works. Occasionally, some people may use the word "profiling" to describe authorities suspecting someone of a crime or otherwise treating someone differently based merely on the person's creed, national origin, race, ethnicity, etc. This practice is not appropriate in locating perpetrators and is typically referred to as racial or religious profiling.

In the real world, unlike in some fictional accounts, offender profiling is not generally the tool authorities use to identify a specific perpetrator. Normally, it is a method authorities use to winnow down the field of suspects. A discussion of the history of the theories behind Offender Profiling and the history of its actual use helps to clarify what, exactly, Offender Profiling is and how it is used. Below are some examples of what offender profiling is, how it came about and where it all began.

Criminal Profiling:

It is "the process of inferring distinctive personality characteristics of individuals responsible for committing criminal acts" (Turvey, 1999).[1]

- Is based on the notion that the crime scene reflects the "psychopathology of the offender" (Holmes & Holmes, 2012).[2]

- Involves presenting a "logical argument regarding the characteristics of an offender responsible for a particular crime or series of crimes" (Turvey, p. 121).

---

[1] Turvey, B. (1999) Criminal Profiling: An Introduction to Behavioral Evidence Analysis, London: Academic Press.
[2] Holmes & Holmes, 2012- Profiling Violent Crimes: An Investigative Tool

Introduction to Offender Profiling

- Is an educated attempt to provide specific information about a suspect and biographical sketch of trends, tendencies, and behavioural patterns (Wrightsman, 2001).[3]

History of Criminal Profiling

Criminal profiling has its roots as far back as the 1800's

In 1876 – Cesare Lombroso stated that many criminals share common physical characteristics:

- Abnormally large head size
- Extremely large jaw/ cheekbones
- Large, pronounced lips
- Extremely long arms
- Abnormal chin (very long, short, or flat)
- Abnormal size and shape of ears[4]

In 1890 after years of research on criminals **Lombroso furthered his profiling into three types of criminals**

1. <u>Born Criminals:</u> Predisposed from birth

2. <u>Insane Criminals:</u> Mental/physical disorders

---

[3] Wrightsman (2001), Forensic Psychology
[4] https://staff.rockwood.k12.mo.us/

3. <u>Criminaloids:</u> No specific characters – yet mental/ emotional states make them dangerous[5]

Jack the Ripper: Insane, quiet, middle aged, nicely dressed

After Lambroso's theories in the late 1800's a new breed of theory arose called Phrenology, [6]this theory determined that a person's personality could be told by the shape of their head and the bumps and fissures of the skull.

The differences between forensic psychology and profiling.

Forensic Psychology is the application of science and psychology to the legal process. (Determination of sanity)

Profiling (Investigative Psychology) deals with the application of psychology to criminal investigations.[7]

---

[5] http://www.practicalethics.ox.ac.uk/__data/assets/pdf_file/0019/30556/Savulescu_paper.pdf
[6] Hartan 2007 - mrhartansscienceclass.pbworks.com/
[7] Criminal Psychology -http://en.wikipedia.org/wiki/Criminal_psychology

Introduction to Offender Profiling

What makes a serial offender?

Developmental Problems:

Focusing on the early developmental years of serial killers has proved a promising approach to explaining the behaviour of these people.

A common feature among sexually motivated multiple murderers is the failure to bond or form an attachment with the parents or primary carer, resulting in a child that appeared to be emotionally detached (Burgess et al, 1985)[8]. Jeffrey Dahmer who by the age of 14 was already having fantasies about killing men and having sex with their corpses, may be cited as an example in this context.

Other examples of disturbed childhood behaviour found in the backgrounds of sadistic serial killers include enuresis, starting fires, and torturing animals.

One difficulty with this theoretical approach is that there are many examples serial killers who have apparently come from quite "normal" respectable backgrounds.

Jenkins. P (1988)[9] found that his research of 12 English serial killers he studied, found that six of them seemed to have quite ordinary childhoods.

---

[8] Burgess, T. L., Craik, C. S. and Kelly, R. B. (1985). The exocrine protein trypsinogen is targeted into the secretory granules of an endocrine cell line: studies by gene transfer. J. Cell Biol. 101, 639-645.
[9] Jenkins, P. (1988) Serial murder in England 1940-1985. Journal of Criminal Justice

Introduction to Offender Profiling

A similar view, Stone (1994)[10] who looked at 42 serial killers, found that while a history of abuse and neglect in childhood was common, 30% of his sample had no such history.

- Thus it seems that while a disturbed upbringing may be a sufficient condition to predispose certain people to multiple murder, it is rarely a necessary condition.

- Violent adults very often will have suffered abuse as children, but only a small proportion of abused children go on to become violent offenders let alone serial killers.

---

[10] Stone, M.H. (1994) Early traumatic factors in the lives or serial murderers. American Journal of Forensic Psychiatry

Introduction to Offender Profiling

Mental illness and serial offending

Are serial killers mentally ill? Surely for a person to commit random acts of multiple murder they must be suffering from some sort of mental illness.

Whilst this explanation may appear to take the easy route to an explanation, the evidence suggests differently. Henn (1976)[11] looked at the psychiatric assessments of 2000 people who had been arrested for murder between 1964 and 1973. Of these, only 1% was found to be psychotic. Mental illness is probably more likely in mass murderers rather than the serial killer and as we have seen, these people are more likely to kill themselves.

One way in which some people cope with severe childhood abuse is to adopt alternative personalities, this is known as a dissociative disorder and often results in the individual having multiple personalities.[12]

Take for instance, one of the hillside stranglers, Kenneth Bianchi, he claimed in his defence that he was suffering from multiple personalities.

While his assessment was being conducted he was put under hypnosis and another one of his personalities came forward, this personality was called, Steve Walker, this alternative personality was described as cold, and vicious and was responsible for the murder of 12 young women. Kenneth Bianchi himself, on the

---

[11] Henn, F., Herjanic, M., and Vanderpearl, R. (1976) Forensic psychiatry: diagnosis and criminal responsibility. Journal of Nervous and Mental Disease
[12] http://www.psychint.net/psychology/psych2000/psych2000/forensic.htm

surface appeared as a nice person, a kind loving husband and father, and he did have any history of being abused by his mother.

After these assessments the psychologist conducting the interviews believed that Bianchi was fabricating the multiple personalities to get out of the charges, this was later proved.

Introduction to Offender Profiling

Psychopathy and serial offending

In defining a psychopath some psychologists define the meaning as someone who exhibits a variety of antisocial behaviours, including violence, and who shows no hint of guilt or regret for their behaviour.

- To a casual observer, the psychopath may appear quite normal, indeed in some cases even charming and this of course is why they can be so dangerous.

- Psychopaths seek total control over situations and individuals and if this control is threatened in any way they may become violent and even murderous.

- The fictional character Hannibal Lector would be a good example of a psychopath.

- Explaining psychopathic behaviour is extremely difficult. [13]

- Attempts at finding a physiological or genetic component have produced inconsistent findings (Raine, A 1989).[14]

There are some professionals in the psychological profession that suggest psychopaths may be less sympathetic to facial cues of anguish, but whether this is a cause of the condition or simply a symptom remains unclear (Blair et al,

---

[13] IBID
[14] Raine, A. (1989) Evoked potentials and psychopathy. International Journal of Psychophysiology

1997[15]). Seto et al (1997)[16] have also observed that psychopaths are far more likely to use deception, even if in some circumstances it is not necessary.

Psychopathy Vs Reactive Offender (whether the offender is a psychopath or if they are reacting to a situation causing the offender to portray specific behaviour)

Psychopaths usually portray:

- Invulnerable
- Superiority

Psychopaths see others as:

- Stupid
- Inferior
- Weak

Psychopaths use strategies like:

- Manipulation
- Violence

Reactive offenders usually portray:

- Vulnerable
- Fluctuates/unstable
- Fragile rights

---

[15] Blair, R.J.R., Jones, L., Clark, E. and Smith, M. (1997) The psychopathic individual: a lack of responsiveness to distress cues? Psychophysiology
[16] Seto, M.C., Khattar, N.A., Lallumiere, M.L. and Quinsey, V.L. (1997) Deception and sexual straegy in psychopathy. Personality and Individual Differences,

Introduction to Offender Profiling

Reactive offenders see others as:

- Hostile
- Oppositional
- The enemy [17]

The odds of meeting your end at the hands of a serial killer in the UK are [18]

- 1 in 1 million (Hicky 1991)

    The odds of winning the lottery are

- 1 in 13 million

So you are more likely to fall victim to a serial killer than you are to win the lottery!

---

[17] http://www.syracusebiotechnology.com/wp-content/uploads/2013/08/Criminal-Profiling-Notes.pdf
[18] www.psychint.net/forensic/serialkillers

Introduction to Offender Profiling

Probably one of the most disturbing aspects of the serial murderer is that they are often so ordinary; indeed it is this ordinariness that allows them to continue with their killing without being detected. e.g. Peter Sutcliffe, the "Yorkshire Ripper" was married to Sonia and had friends and family none of whom initially suspected.[19]

In the USA, John Wayne Gacy was a respected member of the community with his own building company, he also tortured, raped, and killed more than 30 men before and burying their bodies under his house.

Statistically, we know who serial killers are likely to be, they will be white males in their late twenties or early thirties, if they are employed it will probably be a blue-collar job, i.e. semiskilled or skilled. Unfortunately this stereotypical description also accounts for a major part of the male population and therefore is of little practical use. A more thoughtful insight into their motivations and behaviours is required before any useful profile can be constructed.

---

[19] http://www.psychint.net/psychology/psych2000/psych2000/forensic.htm#serial

Introduction to Offender Profiling

Typologies of killers

It is possible to put serial murderers into different types, these types or typologies based on various criteria (Harrower, 1998)[20]. These typologies are often based on motivation or modus operendi, i.e. the specific methods used by the killers. Holmes and DeBurger (1988)[21] suggest four types of serial killer:

Visionary .... these people kill for some "higher" reason, perhaps a religious belief, of because voices tell them they should. These types of killers are often considered to be mentally ill, suffering from a psychotic delusion.

David Berkowitz, the Son of Sam, shot 13 people and killed 6 because he was told to by Satan in the form of a black Labrador dog.

Mission-Orientated ....these people see themselves as having a mission in life, usually to rid the world of some particular group of people, e.g. prostitutes or children; Peter Sutcliffe the Yorkshire Ripper is an example.

Power/Control.... types are people whose murderous behaviour may have a sexual basis but who also have a strong need to exert control over others often to the point of death. Fred and Rosemary West appear to be of this type, often binding their victims to make them totally helpless before torturing and killing them.

---

[20] Harrower, J (1998) Applying Psychology to Crime. Hodder and Stoughton
[21] Holmes, R., and DeBurger, J. (1988) Serial Murder. Newbury Park:

Introduction to Offender Profiling

Hedonists .... are killers who derive some form of pleasure or satisfaction from the murders. The pleasure may be direct as in the case of those who have sexual or sadistic motives, or it may be indirect, e,g, they may gain financial benefits from those they kill, e.g. John George Haigh, the acid bath murderer who killed six people and dissolved their bodies in a bath of acid, believing that without a body murder could never be proved.

Predatory Agression

- No perceived threat
- Goal oriented
- No conscious experience of emotion
- Planned, purposeful violence
- Increased self-esteem
- Unimpaired reality testing
- Generally associated with males and masculinity[22]

---

[22] http://proz.ontodo.org/presentations/234253/index.html?page=6

Affective Agression

- Perceived threat
- Goal threat reduction
- Conscious experience of emotion
- Reactive, unplanned violence
- Decreased self-esteem
- Possible loss of reality testing
- Generally associated with females and femininity[23]

Obviously the criteria used to form typologies will vary with different researchers and there may well be overlaps between the typologies developed.

Hickey (1986)[24] focused on the mobility of the serial killer and identified three types on this basis:

Those killers who have very little mobility and therefore choose their victims from their immediate locations, i.e. their own homes, places of work or surrounding streets. The victims of the Moors Murderers all lived within a few streets of the killers.

A moderate degree of mobility allows the killer to venture further afield, although in the case of this research this was restricted to the home state of the killer. In the UK, John Duffy the "Railway Rapist" would be an example of this. He murdered three women and raped 18 more. His victims were all found close to a

---

[23] Meloy (1988). The Psychopathic Mind. Jason Aronson.
[24] Hickey, E. (1986) Serial Murderers and their Victims. Belmont:Wadsworth

railway station. John Duffy worked for the railways. He was caught following the intervention of David Canter, a Criminal psychologist who produced an offender profile that predicted the murderer would live or work close to a railway line.

The highly mobile killers are those who will travel across states (in the USA) as they kill, and who for this reason are often difficult to catch. Hicky (1986)[25] suggests that the highly mobile killer is probably in the minority with only 32–35% of all victims being killed by this sort of murderer.

In the UK Robert Black, a convicted child killer was a van driver who spent a lot of his time driving from London to Scotland. The bodies of his victims were found close to the route he used to take.

---

[25] Hickey, E. (1986) Serial Murderers and their Victims. Belmont:Wadsworth

Introduction to Offender Profiling

Techniques used in criminal profiling.

Stages in profiling

1. Input: Collecting info about the crime.

2. Decision process models: Data is organized and classified. Determine motives. Victimology.

3. Crime assessment: Crime reconstruction. Modus Operandi (MO) and Signature.

4. Criminal profile: Describing the suspect.

5. Investigation: Report is given to investigators.

6. Apprehension: (hopefully)

"The logic is, that the way a person thinks, guides his or her behaviour"

Profiling, according to Jackson and Bekerian (1997)[26] can take several forms:

Offender profiling is the collection of empirical data in order to collate a picture of the characteristics of people involved in certain types of crime, e.g. is there a typical rapist or serial killer?

---

[26] Jackson, J. L., & Bekerian, D. A. (1997). Does Offender Profiling Have a Role to Play? In J. L. Jackson, & D. A. Bekerian, Offender Profiling: Theory, Research and Practice (pp. 1-7). Chichester: Wiley

Introduction to Offender Profiling

Crime scene profiling uses information from the crime scene; this may include forensic evidence or statements by the victim or witnesses, to build a picture of the offender.

Psychological profiling uses standardised personality measures sometimes coupled with interviews to examine the extent to which a suspect might fit the personality type of a particular type of offender, e.g. rapist.

Introduction to Offender Profiling

Paraphilias

For many serial killers murder alone is not enough, they need to degrade, torture, and humiliate their victims....an expression of their need for control. For this reason there is often an element of sexual sadism in the way they kill their victims. Sexual sadism is an example of a paraphilia.... it is defined in the Diagnostic and Statistical Manual IV as "acts in which psychological or physical suffering of the victim is sexually exciting, including domination or torture". [27]

- Paraphilias are usually described as unnatural sexual acts or perversions and include necrophilia (sex with corpses), zoophilia (sex with animals) and paedophilia (sex with children).

- It is not uncommon to find multiple paraphilias within the same individual.

- Brittain (1970)[28] suggests that the sadistic murderer often feels inferior to others, may find it difficult to form relationships with women and has an almost uncontrollable desire for power over others.

- This type of killer will use fantasy to help him cope with feelings of inadequacy and ultimately may act out these fantasies.

- They are likely to feel sexually aroused as a result of the fear expressed by their victims.

---

[27] http://www.psychint.net/psychology/psych2000/psych2000/forensic.htm#serial
[28] Brittain, R.P. (1970) The sadistic murderer. Medicine, Science and the Law

Introduction to Offender Profiling

- Fred and Rosemary West are good examples of the sexual sadist.

Their victims were rendered helpless by tying them very elaborately with a variety of ropes. Their heads were wrapped in cling film with a thin pipe allowing them to breathe. They were then systematically tortured before being murdered.

Introduction to Offender Profiling
Psychological profiling and psychologists steps in profiling

The criminal psychologist in investigating crimes will take the follow details into consideration, the details which the profiler will take into consideration are:

- Location: Indoor, outdoor, vehicle, underwater etc. – who frequents the location, how can it be reached, what normal activities, why there etc?

- Victimology: Why did offender choose victim?

- Crime Scene type: point of contact & primary, secondary, intermediate & victim disposal sites

- Method of approach: Surprise, con or blitz

- Method of attack: initial means for overpowering a victim.

- Method of control: controlled force; verbal or non-verbalized threats, [includes sexual threats] – the amount of force used can help determine the offenders needs & motives.

Psychoanalysis in criminal profiling

It has been suggested that sexual sadism may result from a fixation at the psychosexual stages of development (Kline, 1987).[29] Degradation of females is an example of reaction formation against the incestuous desires for the opposite sex parent (Oedipus complex, describe a boy's feelings of desire for his mother and jealously and anger towards his father, and Electra complex, describe a girl's sense of competition with her mother for the affections of her father).

By subjecting females (mother substitutes) to violence and degrading acts the sadist is refusing to acknowledge the sexual feelings that they have for their mother.

Anal fixation which is a result of inadequate toilet training can result in buggery, a common feature of sexual sadism.

Gallagher (1987)[30] suggests that a dysfunctional parent–child relationship will lead to the child becoming fixated at an immature stage of development.

The case of Ed Kemper who had a difficult relationship with his domineering mother is often cited as an example. As a result of the feelings of frustration and ambivalence which stemmed from this relationship, by the age of 15 Kemper had killed both his grandparents.

---

[29] Kline, P. (1987) Psychoanalysis and crime. In McGurk, B.J., Thornton, D.M. and Williams, M, (eds) Applying Psychology to Imprisonment: Theory and Practice. London
[30] Gallagher, B.J. III (1987) The Sociology of Mental Illness. Englewood Cliffs: Prentice-Hall

Introduction to Offender Profiling

After his release into his mother's care, and despite the fact that his psychiatrist though he was making good progress, he was in fact murdering female hitchhikers, cutting them up, saving various body parts and cooking and eating others.

Finally he decapitated his mother before having sex with her corpse. He later claimed that this final act had a liberating effect on him so that he no longer felt the need to kill other women.

Ressler et al (1988)[31] have suggested that negative life experiences give rise to aggressive and sexual fantasies which help the individual restore a sense of control in their life.

When they interviewed 36 convicted sex murderers (USA) 25 of who were serial killers they found that 42% had been sexually abused as children and 32% as adolescents. 70% of them felt sexually incompetent and relied heavily on pornography.

Prentky et al (1989)[32] compared serial sex murderers with single sex murderers and found that 86% of the serial killers fantasized prior to the killings compared with only 23% of the single murderers.

---

[31] Ressler, R.K., Burgess, A.W., and Douglas, J. (1988) Sexual Homicide:patterns and Motives. Lexington: Lexington Books
[32] Prentky, R., Burgess, A.W., Rokous, F. et al. (1989) The presumptive role of fantasy in serial sexual homicide. American Journal of Psychiatry

The amount of fantasy was also found to be correlated with the planning and organisation of the murders by the serial killers.

Gresswell and Hollin (1997)[33] go so far as to suggest that fantasy is an addictive process and that serial killers use it to try and regain the sense of euphoria that accompanied the killing of their victims.

Fantasy alone however is never enough and so the serial killer has to seek out further victims.

Fantasy may also be used to try out new features, i.e. ways of torturing or killing the victims, before the actual event.

Based on interviews with 20 serial killers between 1982 and 1991 it was concluded that multiple murder may well be an addictive pattern of behaviour like any other addiction, i.e. serial killers are addicted to killing.

Another method of developing typologies was devised by Ressler, Burgess and Douglas (1988) who were working for the Federal Bureau of Investigation (FBI).

---

[33] Gresswell, D.M., and Hollin, C.R. (1997) Addictions and multiple murder: a behavioural perspective. In Hodge, J., McMurran, M. and Hollin, C. (Eds) Addicted to Crime? Chichester: J

Introduction to Offender Profiling

After extensive research using FBI files on serial killers they came to the conclusion that two types of serial killer could be identified:

- **The Organised Killer**
- **The Disorganised Killer**

The traits of an organised killer

The **Organised** killers were described as being socially competent and intelligent; they were often married and had skilled occupations.

- They would plan their murders, usually targeting strangers, who after restraining they would often have sex with before killing them.
- After the killing the body is usually hidden and any weapons or evidence removed.
- Their crimes often involve the use of a vehicle to transport the victim or move the body.
- They may return to the scene of the crime and are likely to anticipate the sorts of questioning they may have to deal with.
- tend to be high in the birth order of their family, usually an oldest child
- very intelligent
- usually have their lives together
- a series of stressful situations caused them to act out

- Most of them have a live-in partner, are socially adept, and will follow the coverage of their crimes in the media very carefully.[34]

---

[34] Amanda Librizzi
http://www.slideshare.net/eew18?utm_campaign=profiletracking&utm_medium=sssite&utm_source=ssslideview

Introduction to Offender Profiling

Organized crime scene suggests an offender:

- Average or above average IQ
- Employed, usually quite skilled
- Socially competent
- Uses alcohol in commission of crime
- Uses car to drive to crime scene/hunt for victim
- Obsessed with media coverage of his crimes[35]

---

[35] Forensic psychology
http://mrhartanssciencecclass.pbworks.com/w/file/fetch/48080816/Criminal%20Profiling%20PowerPoint.pdf

Introduction to Offender Profiling

The traits of a disorganised killer

The **Disorganised** murderer was described as socially immature; they have a poor work history, are sexually inhibited and may level alone.

- They may live or work near the crime scene and the victims are often known to them.
- The murder is often spontaneous with a great deal of violence.
- Use of restraints is minimal and any sexual acts are likely to occur after the death of the victim.
- The crime scene will show clear evidence of the murder with the body and other evidence simply left with no attempt to hide it, crime scene – random and sloppy.[36]
- Remain detached throughout the course of the crime
- very little conversation, if any, between the offender and victim
- They show no interest in the crime after the event, e.g. won't follow progress of the investigation in the media.
- average or slightly below-average intelligence
- They are younger children, live alone, and are not as socially mature as an organized offender
- Often live or work near the scene of the crime

---

[36] http://www.psychint.net/psychology/psych2000/psych2000/forensic.htm#serial

Introduction to Offender Profiling

Disorganized crime scene suggests an offender:

- Below average IQ
- Unstable employment record, unskilled
- Socially isolated
- Lives close to crime scene
- Strict discipline as a child
- Extremely anxious

If there is a mixture of organized and disorganized offender behaviour it is harder to use criminal profiling for, but it is still possible. For example, the offender may have provided his own tools, but picked a victim randomly.[37]

---

[37] IBID

Introduction to Offender Profiling
Chapter 2- Background and History of Offender Profiling

While the term Offender Profiling is new, the study of how to profile offenders has been used for quite some time. There have been numerous writings on the subject.

One of the earliest books on the subject was written by an Italian Professor of Psychiatry. Professor Lombroso stated that in the 1860s he realized that it may be possible to identify criminals through scientific study. (Fererro, 1911). He realized one possible group of people he could possibly study (as there were ethical concerns and logistical difficulties in completing psychological experiments on humans in most cases), was criminals. He started studying criminals who had been convicted and who had been sentenced in a local prison, and attempted to compare them to the general population, looking for traits that were prevalent among the criminals that were not prevalent in those who had not been convicted of a crime. He came up with several theories, none of which ultimately panned out, but his study of criminals in the 1800s was the first attempt to study criminals systematically. His findings included various traits he thought were prevalent among criminals, including mental illness, certain skull shapes, tattoos, hair growths patterns and even epilepsy. While his findings did not hold up, his study was the first attempt at criminology as we know it. He hypothesized that there were several types of criminals, including born criminals, criminally insane people, and those that he called criminaloids who he stated had some but not all) of the characteristics of born criminals and who may have therefore some choice in the matter of whether or not to become criminals. He discussed methods of preventing crime, including carefully raising orphans and institutionalizing the insane.

Charles Goring, an English Doctor, questioned Lombroso's findings and did a study comparing the traits of thousands of convicts to other individuals (nurses, hospital patients, soldiers and university students). His findings were that "The physical and mental constitution of both criminal and law-abiding persons, of the same age, stature, class and intelligence, are identical." (Goring, 1913). Goring believed that a statistical approach would be more accurate. He did, however, find a relationship between lower than usual intelligence and crime, though in his conclusion he discussed that it was unclear whether that lower intelligence was the cause of the crime, or just another symptom caused by environmental factors. (Goring, 1913)

In the 1930s, Edward Hooten, an American Psychiatrist, completed a study on these issues. He questioned the use of intelligence tests and pointed out that the results were biased. He stated the following in 1936 ""The fitness of any man to live in any community depends on his ability to fall in with its ways. If he is very unadaptable, he is a criminal. He is not blond or dark. He is not tall or short. He is not German or Irish. He is a man who has been woven into American social fabric, who thinks as his fellow citizens do about accepted institutions and who conduct himself as they do. By his deeds is he to be judged: not by his looks or his geographic origin." (1936). Doctor Hooten believed that criminals, not based on any race or national origin, were physically and mentally inferior and he was very interested in using eugenics to attempt to stem crime. Despite this dubious argument, his study of over ten thousand convicts in America was ground-breaking at the time it was done.

Probably the first written work about offender profiling based on psychology was written by Doctor Hans Gross, an Austrian Judge. His work, Criminal Psychology, a Manual for Judges, Practitioners and Students was published in 1893 and first published in English in 1911 (Hans Gross, 1918). Doctor Gross suggested that criminals could be better understood by studying their crimes. He explained that each criminal has a style that they usually do not stray far from. He discussed how having deformities is not the mark of a natural born criminal, as some had previously argued, but that often a person with such deformities likely has been treated poorly from childhood on therefore resulting in behaviour caused by bitterness or jealousy, as opposed to the deformity itself. Doctor Gross was the first to realize that studying a criminal's modus operandi (which is Latin for "way of operating") (The Oxford University Press, 2016), and motives could be useful in solving crime. He started looking at various patterns, and considering things such as the effect that stimuli like economics, upbringing, class, etc., have on causing a person to become a criminal.

Introduction to Offender Profiling
Chapter 3 – History of Use of Offender Profiling

The use of offender profiling seems standard based on what we see when we watch many television shows and movies. Media would give us the impression that a police force of any size would regularly work with Offender Profilers, or even have a profiler or two on staff. However, the actual use of profiling is a newer phenomenon that historically was infrequently used. The idea of using psychology to assist in solving crimes is a relatively new concept.

Introduction to Offender Profiling

Jack the Ripper

The first recorded use of offender profiling in an actual investigation was in the Jack the Ripper case. Several prostitutes were murdered in the Whitehall area of London in August and September of 1888. The murders were extremely brutal with the victims being mutilated by a knife after they were murdered. The police were looking for someone who had some medical knowledge because of the amount of mutilation.

In October of 1888, the police asked their surgeon to provide a report on the murders. He did an autopsy of one of the victims and reviewed the notes from the other investigations in order to write his report. Unlike the police, he did not believe that the murderer had any surgical skills, and suggested he didn't know more about human anatomy than a butcher or horse slaughterer would know. (Bond, 1888). Based on his review of the case he came up with a profile of the suspect. Based on his review he was able to come up with several other characteristics that he thought the police should be looking for. For example, based on the amount of damage and mangling done, he believed that the person would be strong. He believed that the murderer surprised his victims before they were able to cry out. He believed that he likely wore a cloak or something to conceal any blood on his arms after the murders. He believed that the man's appearance would not be unusual because he had not been caught. He also suspected that the person did not have regular employment but had some sort of income, such as a pension and that his neighbours probably had reason to suspect that something wasn't right with him but would likely be scared to come forward, and therefore suggested a reward. He also suggested possible motives.

While this is the first well known recorded use of offender profiling, it was not successful. Jack the Ripper was not identified. Theories as to who the murderer could have been abound even to this day. The story has been retold in the media repeatedly in various forms, some historical, others fictional, and tours of the murder scenes are still available to sightseers in London.

Introduction to Offender Profiling

The Babes of Inglewood

On the afternoon of June 26, 1937, four little girls were playing in Centinela Park in Inglewood California. The play session started out with them running, giggling, playing in the dirt and chasing each other near a large pipe. The fourth girl, Theresa Pinamonti Zeigler, was with her older sister and had to leave before the disappearance occurred. The other three girls, Madeline and Melba Everett and Jeaneatte Steven, all ages 7-9, failed to return home and were reported missing. Police started looking for a kidnapper. Ultimately, the bodies of the three girls were located a few days later. (Zeigler, 2007)

Police questioned nearby adults and arrested a bachelor who lived nearby who had given rides to area children, however, authorities quickly discovered that he was innocent. (Zeigler, 2007). Authorities resumed searching for the suspect. Investigators from Los Angeles joined the search and asked Doctor Joseph Paul de River, a Los Angeles Psychiatrist to help with the investigation. For a few years before that Doctor De River had been assisting the Los Angeles Police Department with some criminal psychiatric cases, initially working with the probation department. (King, 2000). De River had become interested in Criminal Psychology. This was a new field that was not regularly studied at the time. Doctor De River stated as follows:

> *I ran around from jail to jail working with the City Probation Department. I acted as consultant psychiatrist to the Probation*

Department, working with Judge A. A. Scott and a number of other judges, examining any case, any sex case that they would give me to examine and it was entirely gratis. I was devoting my whole time to that because I was pioneering a new field, a field where you can't get post-graduate work in the United States at any medical school or hospital . . . that is criminal psychiatry and I was working that way. I was interested in it. . . . There was nobody interested in the sex degenerate. . . . There was very little written in textbooks by anyone of authority so I went after it in a practical way.
(King, 2000)

Doctor De River looked at the bodies, and the evidence and came up with the following profile:

Look for one man, probably in his twenties, a pedophile who might have been arrested before for annoying children. He is a sadist with a superabundance of curiosity. He is very meticulous and probably now remorseful, as most sadists are very apt to be masochistic after expressing sadism. The slayer may have a religious streak and even become prayerful. Moreover, he is a spectacular type and has done this thing, not on sudden impulse, but as a deliberately planned affair. I am of the opinion that he had obtained the confidence of these little girls. I believe they knew the man and trusted him. (King, 2000)

Introduction to Offender Profiling

The murderer who was ultimately convicted was Albert Dyer. He was a thirty-two-year-old school crossing guard who had helped the girls cross the street by their school. He admitted to planning the murders and even praying over the bodies, just as Doctor De River had predicted. Oddly enough, it was not Doctor Dyer's profile that led to Mr. Dyer's arrest. Mr. Dyer stormed into the police office demanding to know why he was being questioned – after the police had already questioned him and determined that he was not a suspect. At any rate, the Los Angeles Police Department ultimately started a Sex Offender Bureau and hired Doctor De River to head up the department. (King, 2000)

Introduction to Offender Profiling

Adolf Hitler and the OSS

The United States Office of Strategic Services was an entity that was responsible for intelligence for the United States government. In the early 1940s, the government asked Doctor Walter Langer, a Psychoanalyst, to prepare a study of Adolf Hitler to assist policy makers and also in assisting with responding with Hitler's propaganda. With some help from other professionals in the field, Doctor Langer was faced with a challenge – psychoanalysis without ever meeting the subject. They interviewed informants and reviewed publicly available information, such as Mein Kampf and My New Order, both written by Adolf Hitler. (Langer, 1943). This study was initially secret, but later was published as a bestselling book, "The Mind of Adolf Hitler." (Waggoner, 1981)

Doctor Langer produced a thorough report detailing Hitler from several different perspectives including, but not limited to, how he perceived himself, how Germans perceived him, how his associates perceived him and as he knew himself. He used psychological analysis to predict Hitler's anticipated future behaviour. (Langer, 1943). Doctor Langer believed that Hitler was "probably a neurotic psychopath bordering on schizophrenia" (Waggoner, 1981), and discussed all the possible outcomes. He determined that it was probable that as Germany faltered in the war efforts Hitler would become more neurotic, and that there was a high chance he would commit suicide rather than submit to being captured. (Langer, 1943). His predictions proved to be very insightful and accurate, even though the report was published about two years before Hitler's death.

Introduction to Offender Profiling

The Mad Bomber

In November of 1940 a bomb was left in the Edison building in downtown New York, along with a note that stated "Con Edison crooks, this is for you." (The History Channel, 2016). This bomber became known as the "Mad Bomber." The bomber left more bombs, each stronger than the prior, until he sent a note in December of 1941 saying that there would be no more bombs during the war, but threatening Con Edison, the local power company. He refrained from further bombs until the war was over, but continued sending letters to media outlets. In March of 1951, a bomb exploded in Grand Central Station in New York. No one was injured in that bombing, but several more bombs were left around New York that year, including one in the public library. The activity stopped for a few years, but in 1954 he bombed Radio City Music Hall, and in 1955 he bombed Grand Central Station again, and also bombed the RCA building, the Staten Island Ferry and Macy's department store. (The History Channel, 2016).

Over 16 years the Mad Bomber hid many pipe bombs in New York City, twenty-two of which exploded injuring fifteen people. A total of eight pipe bombs had been detonated in subway terminals, causing a great deal of fear. People started to refuse to take the subway and ride only buses, because they thought that was where the Mad Bomber was likely to strike again. Finally, in December of 1956 a bomb exploded in Paramount Theater in Brooklyn and injured six people. The next day, New York's Chief of Police stated that there would be an all-out manhunt. (Delafuente, 2004).

Doctor James Brussel, a Psychiatrist, was brought in to review the evidence and create a criminal profile. He determined that the Mad Bomber was paranoid and becoming worse. He used that to create inferences of possible traits, characteristics. He suspected that the bomber would be middle aged, single, living with female relatives, and wearing a double breasted suit. (NPR News, 2011)

Because of the handwriting on the notes left with some of the bombs, police believed that the bombings had been perpetrated by one person, rather than by a group of people. This belief was due to offender profiling because previous bombings in New York had frequently been done by groups rather than individuals. In December of 1956 the New York Journal-American, a local newspaper, published a letter to the bomber asking him to turn himself in and promising him a fair trial. The bomber responded with a letter refusing to turn himself in and stating that he had suffered an on-the-job injury at Con Edison and complaining that the company failed to compensate him fairly for the injury. The Mad Bomber started writing back and forth with the New York Journal-American. Armed with this bit of information, Con Edison went through employee records, and identified George Metesky, a fifty-three-year-old man who lived with his sisters, as the bomber. Upon arriving, police apprehended Mr.

Metesky, and located bomb making materials. Mr. Metesky admitted the crime, stating he had been injured in an accident and left unable to work, and expressed a great deal of anger towards Con Edison, which had bought the plant where he had been injured. (Delafuente, 2004). Apparently, Mr. Metesky had not been caught for all of those years merely because he appeared to be the typical "next-door neighbour." Mr. Metesky attempted to convince the Court that he was sane because he wanted to go to trial so he could produce evidence that Con Edison had given him Tuberculosis, but he was found to be incompetent and institutionalized. (NPR News, 2011).

Doctor Brussel's profile was not completely accurate, but was accurate in several details. The age was off by about a decade and Mr. Metesky was not arrested in a double breasted suit, merely because he had changed out of his typical suit into his pyjamas at the time the police arrived, but many of the details were accurate, including the offender's mental issues, marital status and living arrangements. Though Doctor Brussel's work may not have been instrumental in the arrest in this case, it really was one of the earlier cases in which offender profiling was used, and Doctor Brussel's methods were followed by others trying to solve crimes using offender profiling thereafter. (NPR News, 2011).

Introduction to Offender Profiling

The Yorkshire Ripper

From 1975 to 1980 several women were attacked in Manchester and Yorkshire England. The attacker bashed the women over the head with a hammer rendering them unconscious, slashed them viscously with a knife and/or a screwdriver and left them bound with clothing removed or moved so as to display certain body parts. In some cases, the perpetrator left semen at the scene. Many, but not all, of the victims were sex workers. There's still speculation that the Yorkshire Ripper may have committed more attacks and may have committed attacks as far away as London. (Tate, 2015). Ultimately, the Yorkshire Ripper was officially credited with 23 brutal attacks, of which 13 were fatal. (Brannen, 2016).

Police attempted to use many of the methods discussed hereinabove to identify and locate the Ripper when it became apparent that the attacks were likely the work of one person. Authorities came up with a profile and began using that to attempt to locate the suspect. The profiling work did not work immediately, in fact the perpetrator was brought in for questioning and cleared repeatedly, but at any rate the profiling methods described above were used. Police used clues such as boot prints, tire tracks and a crisp new five pound note that was traced to one of thirty-five firms using a combination of offender profiling and traditional research to narrow down the group of possible suspects. (Brannen, 2016). Ultimately Peter Sutcliffe, a lorry driver, was arrested and found guilty of the murders. He plead guilty to seven non-lethal attacks. He was sentenced to life in prison in 1981. (Tate, 2015)

This case was an important stepping stone to Offender Profiling as it is used today because there were two new aspects that came into play. The first was the concept of a signature. That concept is simply that when crimes are too similar and unusual to be coincidental, it is as if the criminal has left a mark or signature on the crime so authorities can tie the crimes to the same perpetrator. In this instance, that is why there have been concerns that there were additional victims that were not identified, because there were similar cases further away that were not associated with the Yorkshire Ripper while the investigations were originally completed. This may have been due to the fact that there was no centralized computer system so data was kept separately in each local police station. (Tate, 2015).

More importantly, this case appears to be the first recorded case of used of Offender Profiling to locate the area that the criminal resided in by using a geographic model. The police hired Stewart Kind, who used the locations of the murders to determine where the perpetrator most likely resided. While this was apparently not the item that lead to police identifying Mr. Sutcliffe as the perpetrator, this was the foundation for a ground-breaking new procedure that is in use commonly today. (International Academy of Investigative Psychology, 2016).

Introduction to Offender Profiling
Offender Profiling in the U.S. – The FBI's Behavioral Analysis Unit

In the 1950s Howard Teten worked for a Sheriff's Department and was studying criminology at Berkeley. He started to notice that his course in Abnormal Psychology dovetailed well with his criminology courses and the evidence he was seeing in the field. He later joined the FBI where eventually he started teaching courses to law enforcement officers. During his second class, the officer started discussing cold cases and something one of the officers learned caused him to interview a suspect in one of those cases – and the suspect confessed. Ultimately, the FBI transferred Patrick Mullally, a Special Agent with a Master's Degree in Psychology, to Quantico to teach the classes with Howard Teten. (The Federal Beaureau of Investigation, 2013).

In 1972 the FBI opened a unit at Quantico which included Agents Mullally and Teten, and eventually Robert Ressler, who is often credited with coming up with the term "serial killer" and with developing Offender Profiling in the U.S. as the Supervisory Special Agent in charge of the FBI's Behavioral Science Unit. Agent Ressler believed it was important to understand murderers' motivations. By the late 1970s the FBI began to intentionally combine the study of crime scene evidence, psychology and study of the victims in order to better understand murderers and what drives them. (Guy, 2016).

These agents interviewed thirty-six serial killers and began forming theories about different categories of killers which will be discussed more in detail in following chapters. Agent Ressler profiled John Wayne Gacy and interviewed Ted Bundy and Jeffrey Dahmer. In 1985 the FBI put the Violent Criminal Apprehension Program into place at Quantico. This program created a national database of violent crime so that investigators could see if similar crimes were occurring in different jurisdictions. (Guy, 2016). The FBI's Behavioral Analysis Unit's work in the 1970's is the foundation for Offender Profiling as it is currently used in the United States today.

Introduction to Offender Profiling

Offender Profiling in the UK/Ireland,

David Canter and Identifying the Railway Ripper

In the early 1980s a man had repeatedly attacked and raped women in and around London. In December of 1985 he abducted a 19-year-old female from a train station and murdered her. He continued on his murder spree, even murdering three people on one night in 1985. Most of his attacks were located near railroad tracks, so he was referred to as the "Railway Ripper." He attacked his victims with a knife and tied them up using string. (The History Channel).

Members of the public were quickly becoming concerned for their safety, and the police department brought in Doctor David Canter to assist them with the investigation. Doctor Canter created a profile which described the murderer as a married man who did not have children but who did have a prior police record of domestic violence. He also used Geographical Mapping in a groundbreaking manner to determine that the offender probably lived in the Kilburn area of London. (The History Channel).

Police had collected a list of 5,000 possible suspects when the Railway Ripper struck again. However, the police were able to compare the list of suspects to Doctor Canter's profile. One man, a former railroad worker named John Duffy, was on the list of suspects because he had previously been accused of domestic violence and he appeared to meet Doctor Canter's profile. Investigators quickly were able to match fibre from Mr. Duffy's clothing to fibres collected at the first murder scene. Mr. Duffy was convicted for two of the murders. Later, accomplices of his were found guilty of some of the other murders. Years later Mr. Duffy confessed to several more murders and rapes.

Doctor Canter's profile was ground-breaking in the field of Offender Profiling for multiple reasons. Unlike the majority of the previously mentioned profiles, rather than the profile merely being proved right or wrong by the arrest, the profile was instrumental in helping the police identify and apprehend Mr. Duffy before he could murder again. Additionally, Doctor Cantor created geographic profiling techniques for this case that law enforcement agencies still use today to determine where an offender may live and/or work.

Introduction to Offender Profiling

An Old Idea Finally Comes to Fruition

As you can see, the idea of using Psychological factors to attempt to locate criminals is not a new one. It dates back at least to the late 1800s as evidenced by both the Jack the Ripper case (and a few other cases Doctor Bond worked on that aren't as well-known today) and by the fictional accounts found in Sherlock Holmes. However, modern technology and the field of Psychology have advanced dramatically in that time frame.

Computer databases are used to track crime so that police can look for patterns in crimes located in different jurisdictions. It is no longer necessary to call or visit every jurisdiction around to verify whether or not there have been similar crimes, as the computers can be programmed to help police locate similar cases. Psychology no longer seeks to categorize people by skull shapes or physical deformities, and has come a long way in helping understand the behaviour of criminals and victims. Additionally, Crime Scene Techniques are now sophisticated enough that analysis of the evidence at the scene(s) and of the suspect is much more likely to lead to admissible evidence that can be used to verify that the profile in question. This includes methods such as testing of blood, DNA, cloth fibres, etc., which were not available until recently. All of these advances have helped Offender Profiling rise to the forefront today.

Introduction to Offender Profiling
Chapter 4 – Offender Profiling Today

Overview –How is it Used Today?

Historically profiling was often used in very infamous cases where nothing else has worked. It seemed as if law enforcement thought that using psychology was only worthwhile in certain sorts of cases. Initially, the general train of thought was that profiling would only be helpful in cases like serial murders, or serial rapes. But now it is used in a lot more contexts. Law enforcement and investigators now use Offender Profiling generally, and the work of investigative psychologists and/or methods developed by them specifically, for several reasons.

For example, investigators use those methods to determine what evidence is really relevant. In other words, they help determine what clues at the crime scene (or elsewhere) might give officers a hint as to the type of the person that committed the crime. Offender profiling can also help investigators determine where they should look for information. For example, if the profiler is able to determine what sort of job the person had that may give investigators the ability to search certain databases or contact possible informers or witnesses in the locations where that sort of profession is common. Or, knowing that the offender is likely to have been violent towards family members in the past would make a search of local domestic violence databases relevant. Let's take a look at some Offender Profiling methods and how they are used today.

Introduction to Offender Profiling

Geographical Profiling

If you have watched a lot of television shows about police you may be somewhat familiar with the general idea of this technique. I suspect that many people can picture a television show or two where the police mapped out several crimes and were attempting to determine where the next crime would take place so they could step up patrols in that area, or where they were trying to determine where the perpetrator lived.

The art of attempting to determine where crimes will take place next geographically is called environmental criminology. The art of attempting to determine where an offender lives using Offender Profiling techniques is called geographical profiling. Practitioners start with some of the same theories in both geographical profiling and environmental criminology. For example, it is assumed that if a criminal has the option to do a crime in two different locations and all other factors are equal the criminal would tend to choose the closer location. (R H Bull, 2006 pp. 19-20) They also assume that offenders are making a rational decision when attempting where to commit a crime. For example, if a jewel thief thought it was possible to steal jewels valued at millions of dollars or pounds and get away with it, he would probably be willing to travel significantly to commit the crime. But by the same token, if he thought another heist would only net him enough to buy him groceries for a week he would not be likely to be willing to travel very far. Often, but not always, criminals will avert doing crimes too close to home because they feel it would be too easy to be caught.

David Canter is one of the leading experts in the field of geographical profiling. Professor Canter theorizes that there are two general types of criminals in terms of geography, the Marauder and the Commuter. Both types have what he calls a "haven" in common – that is to say a base of operations such like the offender's home or office. This is where the offender returns to after committing the crimes. (International Academy of Investigative Psychology, 2016).

If you would look at a map of a marauding criminal's crimes, the offender would live or otherwise have his or her safe haven somewhere in the midst of where all the crimes are committed. He or she would tend to commit crimes in a limited area and it would be an area that he or she was familiar with. Often the marauder would tend not to cross psychological borders or cultural borders to commit crimes. For example, a marauder may not cross the street at the edge of a neighbourhood he favours, or he may not cross a bridge out of town. A marauder would commit crimes in areas the marauder knows well and would not travel too far afield. (International Academy of Investigative Psychology, 2016). Often, the criminal may avoid doing crimes too close to one another which ultimately means that the crimes will be dispersed around their haven or home, so that their haven would be somewhere towards the center of the area the crimes were committed. (R H Bull, 2006 p. 21)

Introduction to Offender Profiling

A commuter, on the other hand, would likely travel away from his home (or haven) to commit crimes. His or her crimes could be geographically miles or even continents apart. A prime example would be a serial killer who only kills when out of town on business and may be in areas the commuter is not as familiar or comfortable with. It is even possible that a commuter may commit crimes in jurisdictions that are on different continents, if he or she is able to do so. The commuter generally has some sort of strategy they use to hunt and they rarely will hunt near their haven. (International Academy of Investigative Psychology, 2016). Commuters may travel away from their haven to commit crime because they do not wish to get caught, or they may travel because they are looking for a certain type of victim or target that does not exist in their area. Some crimes tend to be done more by marauders than others, such as serial stranger rapes and serial arson. But any criminal can change types on occasion so investigators cannot always assume any one criminal must always act as a marauder or a commuter. For example, a serial robber could typically be a marauder because he or she usually targets the richest neighbourhood in town, but that doesn't mean that if he or she would not act if they became aware of an easy, lucrative target that is closer to their haven.

One theory that Professor Canter has used with some success is the Circle Theory of Environmental Range. In that theory, the investigator picks the two known offenses that are furthest apart and marks them on a map. The investigator then draws a circle going through both of those points. It is fairly likely, at least in the case of a commuter, that the criminal's residence would be somewhere near the center of that circle. (R H Bull, 2006 p. 22)

There is software readily available that can be used to help investigators geographically profile an offender. There are several programs in existence. A few such as Dragnet, which was developed by Professor Canter, and Predator are used by their developers as part of their own criminal profiling practices. Rigel Analyst is software that is available for law enforcement agencies to purchase. CrimeStat is software that is currently available as a free download over the internet. (Shively, 2004). Offender Profilers use geographic profiling to aid investigators by narrowing down the areas that they need to search for the offender.

Introduction to Offender Profiling

Guiding the Investigation

Offender Profiling can also be used to guide the investigation itself. For example, a profiler may be called upon to look at a crime scene (or multiple crime scenes), autopsy, investigative reports, evidence, etc., and help investigators determine what is relevant from a psychological perspective. While it is patently obvious that certain evidence is relevant to investigators, and even the average citizen (certainly everyone knows a bloody murder weapon is important evidence). However, an Offender Profiler can assist in determining which less obvious clues may be more helpful (or which clues that appear to be important may not be as important as the investigator would assume). In addition, as trained experts on behaviour, they may be able to deduce things about the type of person the investigator is looking for when the investigator is not able to do so.

In addition to helping investigators determine what evidence is relevant, Offender Profilers may be able to use their knowledge of psychology to help investigators know what sources may be useful in locating the offender. For example, an Offender Profiler may be able to look at evidence and determine that it is likely that the perpetrator had been arrested for domestic violence in the past the investigators could search databases to look for persons residing near the crime who have had such convictions. In some situations, an Offender

Introduction to Offender Profiling

Profiler may be able to give investigators an idea of not only previous crimes, but also how those were committed.

They can also give investigators an idea of what sort of person they are looking for. For example, for example, they may be able to give the investigator clues as to the temperament of the offender and what sort of things may be triggers for the offender. This information would give investigators clues as to the behaviour of the person they are looking for which can help them focus in on suspects matching the behavioural patterns. Additionally, the profiler may be able to determine things such as the level of education, mental health, habits, etc., all of which can help point the investigators to the correct suspect and eliminate people who do not match the profile. Additionally, profilers may be able to look at behavioural clues to determine things like when and where the criminal is likely to strike next, and whether or not the offender is likely to commit more violent or different crimes.

Introduction to Offender Profiling

Crime Linkage

This is another area where Offender Profiling can assist investigators. Let's say that a string of murders occurs in a metropolitan area over a period of several months. The murders are all similar but not identical. The murders in question were gruesome and attracted a lot of media attention. Investigators would need to determine how many suspects to look for. Are the murders the work of one person, or maybe a few people working together? Or were some of the murders copycat murders? Did the offender commit similar crimes elsewhere?

This process is known as crime linkage. This is something that has been challenging for investigators historically. Speculation as to whether or not some of the famous serial killers we discussed earlier may have committed other crimes is rampant. Sometimes this is the result of investigators becoming aware of similar crime after the fact (particularly before the use of computer databases that allow investigators to track violent crimes across different jurisdictions) and other times this can come up when the offender tells people there were more victims. There is speculation that Jack the Ripper and the Yorkshire Ripper committed murders that were not attributed to them at the time the murders were committed. In fact, a newspaper article was published as recently as 2015 suggesting that the Yorkshire Ripper may have murdered another young girl. (Parveen, 2015).

Introduction to Offender Profiling

Sometimes, watching crime procedurals in media, we can get the idea that a serial murderer always murders in exactly the same way so that it is patently obvious to the investigator whether or not the same murdered committed the crime by merely looking at the crime scene. But the reality is, serial criminals they may not always use the same weapon, methods, stage the site the same, etc. While some criminals may have a specific pattern that acts as a signature, tying the crime to the same person, others do not. Even those that do may not always be able to complete their act or may not have access to the same weapon. Consider a murderer who likes to stage victims, but who is unable to finish in one case because he is interrupted before he gets a chance to finish his work. In a situation like this, evidence of the offender's signature behaviour may be missing. Investigators who are trained to look at the evidence may not realize that the crimes are linked (committed by the same offender) but a profiler may be able to look at the evidence and determine that the crimes were related but that the offender was interrupted. By the same token, a profiler may be able to determine that two crime scenes that appear on the face of things to be linked are not by considering evidence of the offender's personality type, etc., that wouldn't be obvious to someone without extensive psychological training.

Introduction to Offender Profiling

Categorisation

One of the most commonly referenced psychological profiling methods referenced is determining whether the crime was of an organized or a disorganized nature. This was initially only applied to serial murders, but later was applied to serial arsons and serial sex offenders as well. The theory is that offenders who are organized plan their attacks, are more likely stage the evidence, are more likely to pick victims they do not know and are less likely to lose control of their temper at the crime scene. The organized offender would be more likely to feel out of control in life, i.e., someone who has financial or family challenges that they feel are beyond their control. They tend to be very controlled about what they say, and much more likely to hide evidence such as the murder weapon and certainly try to remove as much evidence from the scene as possible. They tend to like to control conversations.

The disorganized offender, on the other hand, is less likely to have planned out things. They may leave evidence out in the open. The disorganized criminal wouldn't stage a body and often will leave the weapon and other evidence at the crime scene. They may tend to be socially awkward and not very talkative. Their crimes tend to be crimes of opportunity or passion and they often knew the victim before the crime. They are more likely to commit sex acts on a victim after the death. This offender may be more manic and less predictable. The disorganized offender is more likely to be driven by mental illness.

While this dichotomy of organized versus disorganized seems to be heavily discussed, its accuracy has not been studied in great detail. Several leading experts in the field have discussed the need for additional categories, or have questioned whether the organized versus disorganized classification is even relevant. There does seem to be agreement that it is common for a serial murderer to sometimes exhibit behaviours consistent with both categories. However, this dichotomy is often used to give investigators a starting point. In 2004, Doctor Canter and his team published a study and determined that the dichotomy of organized versus disorganized is not really definitive and suggested that by definition all serial killers can be considered at least somewhat organized by the serial nature of their crimes. (David V. Canter, 2004).

This doesn't mean that the theory is irrelevant, however. Rather, the FBI has now taken the approach that the serial criminal will fall somewhere on the spectrum between highly organized and highly disorganized. This enables investigators, working closely with psychologists, to help determine what sort of a person committed a series of crimes. (Winerman, 2004). Having an understanding of the offender's psychological profile enables investigators to know what sort of person they are looking for, so that as they start interviewing suspects they have an idea who they are looking for.

Introduction to Offender Profiling
Chapter 5 – Serial killers, spree killers, mass killers

Leyton (1986) argues that in order to understand the phenomenon of serial killing factors beyond the psychological tradition need to be analysed. His structural account using evidence of American serial killing and focusing on socio-economic factors provides a powerful contribution to a neglected area. Leyton, E. (1986)

The phrase, "serial killer," was first used in a book, The Complete Detective, in 1950, (Wormser, R 1950) while serienmörder was coined in 1931 in Germany in reference to Peter Kürten (a German serial killer known as both The Vampire of Düsseldorf and the Düsseldorf Monster).

In some states in the USA serial killers are classified as "Three or more separate events in three or more separate locations with an emotional cooling off period in between murders.", whereas in the UK and Ireland "some" scholars define as "two or more separate events in separate locations with a time lapse between and no relationship between the murderer and victim".

Egger. S, (1984) suggests a six point identification of the serial killer: there must be at least two victims; there is no relationship between perpetrator and victim; the murders are committed at different times and have no direct connection to previous or following murders; the murders occur at different locations; the murders are not committed for material gain; subsequent victims have characteristics in common with earlier victims. This definition is challenged by Souns. H, 1995, who claimed that the definition was too restrictive and allowed some heinous killers to fall outside his definition such as Fred and Rosemary West, they are not "technically" serial killers as they killed all of their victims at the same address in Glouster, England. They only had a relationship with one of their victims, their daughter Heather, setting them outside this "definition".

In the USA the definition was coined by Douglas et al. (1992) "...three or more separate events in three or more separate locations with an emotional cooling-off period between homicides. The serial murder is hypothesized to be premeditated, involving offense-related fantasy and detailed planning". This definition has now been reduced officially by the FBI to "Serial Murder: The unlawful killing of two or more victims by the same offender(s), in separate events" (FBI. 2008)

The definitions of Eggar are at the forefront of the investigation of serial killers, his work has contributed immensely to the research and study conducted worldwide, but whether the definitions are working in modern times is yet to be proven.

Other definitions on the "three or more victims" comes from the following; (Hickey. S.W 1997) "...an offender had been charged with killing three or more individuals over a period of days, weeks, months, or years..." and "...the homicides had to be deliberate, premeditated acts whereby the offender selected his or her own victims and acted under his or her own volition" . Holmes & Holmes (1994) "A serial killer is defined as someone who murders three persons in more than a 30-day period. These killings typically involve one victim per episode".

But the consensus is now that the number of people the perpetrator murders, is internationally recognised as "two victims" to me a serial killer.

Serial killer V Mass Killer V Spree Killer

There is a further breakdown of the killing of more than two persons which can at least confuse the lay person, a serial killer is now defined as the killing of two or more persons by the same offender in separate events, Serial killers are not the same as mass murderers, who commit multiple murders at one time; nor are they spree killers, who commit murders in two or more locations with virtually no break in between,(serial killers have the "cooling off" period) whereas the definition of mass murderer is the murder of two or more persons at the same time in the same location by the same person, Dennis Rader ("B.T.K.") started his killing with the killing of his family, "four in the same spree", which made him a mass murderer. He then killed several single women over a span of several decades. Although he is a mass murderer he is not known as such, he is known as a serial killer, when in fact he is both.

If this is the case the so called "family 'annihilations' which take place in Ireland are mass murder, but alas, they are not known as such, maybe this is due to the inability of people to take in the immensity and gravity of what happened. Professor (Wilson. D, 2013), "The research defined family annihilation as where a parent — predominantly a father — kills his children, and frequently his partner or ex-partner, and typically attempts to kill himself, usually successfully." (Wilson. D, 2012)

Introduction to Offender Profiling

Family annihilations are Mass murder

In order to understand the phenomenon at least here in Ireland anyway we need to look at the types of annihilators. This is not an exhaustive list it is a list compiled by Professor Wilson and his team in Birmingham City University which concluded in 2012.

(Wilson. D, 2012) and his team found as follows;

The team identified four different types of annihilators.

There are the "self-righteous", who, according to Prof Wilson, are the most common type, who seek to blame the partner or ex-partner.

They are often "very controlling, very narcissistic, and dramatic". He said they often take their own lives because they don't want the criminal justice system to judge them.

A second type are "paranoid", those who see an external threat, which can either be real or imagined. Prof Wilson said examples include the possibility of social services taking the children, resulting in the dad killing his children instead.

A third type are the "disappointed" — those who feel they have been "let down" by the family for failing to fulfil a view of what the family should be.

Introduction to Offender Profiling

The fourth type is the "anomic" type, those who have lost their source of income. Prof Wilson said these are men who "typically have some status, with professional acumen and with some success in business".

The findings showed that these "usually" men felt that they no longer had a family so there was no point in its existence. If they could not control it then it would not BE. It also found that if those who had killed their family could not face the outside world with their failures so annihilated the family and themselves to save face.

"What link the four types are masculinity and the changing nature of man and changing nature of woman in society," (Wilson. D, 2012) . There are also four types of reasons why serial killers start their spree of killing.

Introduction to Offender Profiling

Serial killers can be defined as;

A person (usually a white male) who enjoys enticing, attacking and murdering his victim, this is done to a strict ritual whereby the killer has his own set routine and array of tools for his/her attack and an organised plan (organised killer) or no plan (disorganised killer). Interestingly enough, in spite of the fact that when they are caught the reasons that drove them to kill another human being appears normal, it is necessary to point out that these killers can be classified into three categories based on the murder motifs, more exactly as lust, missionary and visionary serial killers.

Introduction to Offender Profiling
The top 10 characteristics of a serial killer

Based upon 36 incarcerated serial killers interviewed by FBI agent Robert Ressler, who was an FBI agent and part of the first (Behaviour Analysis Unit BAU), He was influential in development of Vi-CAP (Violent Criminal Apprehension Program), Serial killers tended to be either Psychopaths,("primary Psychopath", a genetic mental personality disorder, physiological defect in the brain responsible for impulse control and emotions.) and Sociopath ("secondary psychopath", an environmentally contributed mental personality disorder, usually as a result of early childhood traumas and abuse) both Antisocial Personality Disorders (ASPD),

Sociopaths incline to be nervous and easily agitated.

They are more so than not uneducated and live on the borders of society, unable to hold down a steady job or live in one place for long. Also, a few sociopaths form attachments to people or group, (they feel empathy for those they form attachments to) although they have no regard for society in general. To the public at large a sociopath appears undoubtedly troubled. Any crimes committed by a sociopath tend to be disorganized and spontaneous.(unorganised serial killers)

Psychopaths, on the other hand, often have charming personalities. They are manipulative and easily gain people's trust. They have learned to mimic emotion and so appear "normal" to other people. Psychopaths are often educated and hold steady jobs. Some are so good at manipulation and mimicry that they can have families and other long-term relationships without those around them ever suspecting their true nature.(very organised and plan any crime to the last detail.) (Organised serial killers.) Ressler was responsible for the compilation of the top 10 traits exhibited by a serial killer and his findings are as follows;

1. *Cruelty to animals*

In approx. 995 of incarcerated serial killers there is a history of animal cruelty which started in childhood.

2. *Abused as children*

The majority of serial killers were abused as children, physically, sexually and emotionally. Serial killers tended to have parents (usually mothers) who humiliated and psychologically abused them.

3. *Wet the bed*

Most serial killers tended to have wet the bed well into late childhood, even into teens.

4. *Narcissistic*

Serial killers often exhibited narcissistic tendencies. They fantasised creating mayhem, trauma and destruction and this often came about by the need to have total control.

5. *Pyromania*

Serial killers are often pyromaniacs; this is believed to be because of their need for control. Often it is used as the serial killers "dummy run" at murder, insofar as they may set a fire and kill animals in a shed etc, in order to estimate damage, feelings and control etc.

6. *Impotent*

It can be said that the lack of relationships in the psychopaths lives can stem from the way they can move around a lot, this can impact their ability to form relationships therefore causing a detachment from emotions of a relationship, further isolating themselves and further making other people "objects".

7. *Developing voyeurism and fetishism in adulthood*

Many serial killers are intensely interested in voyeurism and fetishism as well as other paraphilia's. Many will start their deviancy as relatively harmless peeping-toms, before moving on to house-breaking, rape, and murder.

8. *Brain Trauma*

Many serial killers suffered head traumas in childhood which resulted in swelling. 70% of serial killers received extensive head injuries as children or adolescents, clearly showing the link between these types of injuries and serial murder. (Listverse, 2012)

9. *Dysfunctional families*

Many serial killers grow up in homes which exhibited dysfunction. Alcohol and drug abuse also encourage delinquency as well as loneliness and isolation.

10. *Alcohol and drug abuse*

Children who are exposed to alcohol and substance abuse in the womb may suffer from serious birth defects. Small eye openings, retardation, a small head and brain and central nervous system issues are just some of the problems they could face, if they survive. (Listverse, 2012)

Introduction to Offender Profiling

Ireland's Serial Killers

Ireland has only two serial killing according to Eggar and the FBI's definitions insofar as it has only one set of killings attributed to the same killer(s) with the death of "two victims". But according to Holmes & Holmes and Hickey Ireland has had NO serial killing in its history.

This is because the largest number of victims from one perpetrator(s) is two. In Ireland there has been two cases of convicted serial killer(s), they were Geoffrey Evan and John Shaw, and Patrick Bambrick. Evans and Shaw came to Ireland in 1974 and intended to kill one woman per week, they were captured after killing two women (Elizabeth Plunkett and Mary Duffy) in Wicklow and Galway, they were caught after the car they had stolen was stopped by Gardai after a shopkeeper in Ma'am in Galway thought the car was suspicious and the two gentlemen had English accents and the car looked suspicious with its bad paintjob. Gardai stopped the car two weeks later after getting the number from the shopkeeper. The two were tried and convicted and sentenced to life in prison, Evans died in 2012 and Shaw is still incarcerated in Castlerea prison.

There is serial killer named Michael Bambrick, who killed of two young women in the early Nineties. Patricia McGawley, 42, and Mary Cummins, 36, both had been simply recorded as "missing persons" until Garda management ordered a review of all Ireland's missing-women cases in the aftermath of the disappearance of another young woman named Annie McCarrick, this review found that Bambrick had been dating both of the missing girls at the time of their disappearance.

After a drinking session which resulted in Bambrick and Patricia becoming involved in a bondage session Bambrick Strangled Patricia who he shared his home with. In a surreal twist, Bambrick then put on Patricia's clothes, lipstick and heels and strolled around St Ronan's Park. He was spotted by suspicious neighbours -- but they weren't aware of what he had just done. Bambrick, had stuffed the body into the spare room in their home and even brought their daughter to school before coming back to dispose of the body.

The killer used a knife and a hacksaw to dismember Patricia's body, removing her head, arms and legs. He then cycled, with the remains in a bag, to an illegal dump at Balgaddy, Lucan, and buried the body parts. A day later he made a second bike trip to the dump, this time with Patricia's torso.

On July 23, 1992 after another drinking session Bambrick met Mary Cummins and plied her with drink, after this he partook in a bondage session but this ended in Bambrick stuffing Mary's tights into her mouth which suffocated her.

In Ireland today there are a number of missing girls throughout the country, it is believed some of those may have been the victim of a serial killer, there is one suspect which is still believed to be the perpetrator unfortunately there has been no definitive proof that he committed these murders but abductions/missing stopped with his incarceration coincided say some, circumstantial say others.

Larry Murphy was arrested for the abduction and rape in February 2000 Murphy, from Baltinglass, Co Wicklow, attacked his victim in a car park in Carlow. He put her into the boot of his car while pretending to be unable to load shopping, his victim tried to aid and he pushed her into the boot, he continued to the Wicklow mountains where he raped her and attempted to kill her by wrapping a plastic bag around her head, he was disturbed by two hunters and ran, he was later caught. He has been quizzed several times about the disappearance of three women who were raped, killed and dumped in the Wicklow Mountains. The suspected victims are Jo Jo Dullard, Annie Mc Carrick and Deirdre Jacob.

In 2007 cold-case detectives invited FBI agents from America to look into the cases. They established that the modus operandi was similar to Murphy's actions in the 2000 rape. Murphy was a married man with two children, and had no previous dealings with the Gardai.

Introduction to Offender Profiling

Chapter 6 – Strengths and Weaknesses of Profiling

There are definitely some strengths and weaknesses to Offender Profiling, some of which are more apparent than others. The data is still limited at this time because, despite what police procedural television shows may lead the public to believe, Offender Profiling is a relatively new area that is not used or studied nearly as often as people would expect.

Strengths

The following are some of the strengths of Offender Profiling as it relates to criminal cases.

Geographical Profiling

Geographical profiling is now readily available to law enforcement officers through the use of software programs that they can buy. There have several scholarly articles and a few studies done in regards to geographical profiling.

Geographical profiling, as studied, tends to be more effective in some types of cases than others. For example, geographical profiling does not work well in cases where the criminal is a commuter. Studies have indicated good results with serial burglary and serial murder cases with a significant reduction in the area that needs to be searched. Because this is a newer field, there have been studies comparing and contrasting different methods, including things like the use of different algorithms, and the use of different methods (such as applying insurer like actuarial rules versus human judgment to attempt to determine the location of the offender's likely home base). Many leading practitioners admit that this is an area that can use a lot of improvement as they can learn how to add things like ease of access by transport, land use, etc., into the calculations in order to come up with even more accurate data. Additionally, researchers are attempting to find ways for offender profilers and geographic offender profiling software to help determine if the offender is a marauder, or a commuter, so they know whether or not the software will assist them in locating the offender.

In short, while the methods for geographical profiling continue to improve, this is an area of Offender Profiling that helps police who are investigating crimes. There is a lot of work to be done to optimize the practice, and also some shortfalls that will be discussed herein below, but this is a rather widely accepted tool that, because of the readily available software, is more widely used by investigators than some other forms of offender profiling.

Introduction to Offender Profiling

Winnowing

One issue that is becoming more challenging to law enforcement in this age where so much data is readily available is simply choosing the right data. Law enforcement has had success using offender profiling techniques to help them winnow down the list of possible sources of information, and also the list of possible suspects. For example, an Offender Profiler may be able to use psychology to predict several pieces of data about the offender, such as age, education level, gender, personality type, past criminal behaviour and much, much more, depending on the evidence left behind at the offender's crime scenes.

Of course, this can be combined with traditional law enforcement techniques and geographical profiling to give the investigators an idea of a starting point. For example, if they are searching for a murderer and evidence on the scene only gave them a few hints using traditional police methods, such as maybe hair colour and approximate shoe size, the Profiler may be able to give them other pieces of information so instead of looking for, for example, a large man with black hair, they may be able to narrow the search down to large man, with black hair, living in a certain area, with a college education, who is shy with women, and with prior arrests or convictions for domestic violence. Once a few details are apparent, investigators can begin to use databases to see if they find people matching the description and, once that is completed, they may be able to winnow that list even further by checking to see how many of the suspects may fit the psychological profile and can focus on those persons first.

This is a fairly accepted use of Offender profiling. A few studies and surveys have been done, but there are limitations to those, which will be discussed herein below. However, the FBI cites a few studies saying that investigators believed offender profiling was useful or helpful to investigators more than 80% of the time. (J. Amber Scherer, 2014).

Concerns and Weaknesses

The following are areas of concerns about Offender Profiling when used in the context of criminal investigations.

Lack of Empirical Evidence

Generally speaking, the scientific method is used to come up with data to see whether there is proof that something is working, or not. This is something that can be done in many scientific fields, including, in many cases, psychology. The gold standard for testing like this is called a double blind test – which simply means that neither the tester nor the subject know who is getting a placebo so scientists can't accidentally influence the outcome of the experiment by any bias they may have. Even in situations where double blind testing isn't possible, researchers try to get blind experiments, which still involves the use of a control group. Researchers look to have results that can consistently be re-created.

Introduction to Offender Profiling

However, that sort of testing isn't really possible for studying offender profiling because there is no way to place a control group. This leaves researchers trying to study the results of real world cases to determine whether or not Offender Profiling was successful in those cases. There are some cases where it is clear Offender Profiling was the key to solving the case, but those cases are what science refers to as anecdotal evidence because they are just observations and cannot be readily duplicated. The facts of each case are different, and each criminal is different. Obviously, criminals aren't going to let researchers follow them around witnessing their crimes to test their theories, so much of what the Offender Profiler does is really considered, at this point, to be more of an art than a science. Until and unless there is scientific evidence, there will be some who question the use of Offender Profiling in criminal investigations. Geographical profiling does lend itself somewhat to study after the fact, by comparing how far the offender's base was from what the model(s) projected, but other than that, science cannot be used to verify what an Offender Profiler can do.

Introduction to Offender Profiling

What is Success?

Another challenge in measuring how successful Offender Profiling is, other than inability to complete proper scientific tests, is that there is no set agreement as to what success is. For example, some would argue that Offender Profiling isn't successful if the offender that is ultimately captured doesn't completely fit the profile that the profiler provided. Others would feel that the use of an offender profiler was a success if the profile lead directly to the arrest of the criminal. Others deem the results positive if the profile points the investigators in the right direction, or gives the investigator a new idea or thought that ultimately helps them solve the case. Or maybe, some may feel a profile is helpful if it enables investigators to more effectively interrogate suspects. Or, it may be possible that a profile is helpful in preventing a wrongful conviction. So there is no set result that investigators hope for when they hire a psychologist to come up with an offender profile, and therefore no way to measure those outcomes exactly. (J. Amber Scherer, 2014)

Clearly, some uses of Offender Profiling are not successful. On occasions, the profile may be incorrect and may send investigators looking for the wrong person. Or, law enforcement could perceive that a profile was helpful when it was not. In one study two different groups of law enforcement officers were given profiles and asked whether they would have helped them solve the case, if they were investigating it. Half of the law enforcement officers were given fake profiles that didn't match very well. Interestingly, many of the law enforcement officers believed that the profiles were helpful – even those who had the fake profiles that did not match well. The researchers determined that there is some evidence that investigators are prepared to accept ambiguous statements as fact when provided in the form of an offender profile, just because the Profiler is an expert. (Laurence Allison, 2003).

While some researchers question whether or not Offender Profiling is helpful, the bottom line is that because it is a field where the definition of success varies, and where scientific study options are severely limited, law enforcement officers will determine whether or not they believe Offender Profiling is valid anecdotally. The use of Offender Profiling has increased significantly, as evidenced by the number of people who now prepare such profiles (and the amount of software available), so therefor it is obvious that law enforcement is increasingly feeling that offender profiling is helpful.

Introduction to Offender Profiling

Admissibility and Use in Courtroom

Another weakness of Offender Profiling is that it isn't always admissible or helpful in the courtroom. In terms of admissibility, different jurisdictions have different rules in terms of whether or not a profiler can testify as an expert witness. In the United States the rules vary from state to state and can be different in a federal trial than in a state trial. There are several different rules that are applicable, and oftentimes prosecutors won't know for certain whether or not an Offender Profiler's expert testimony will be admitted until during the trial. Even then, it is possible that only parts of the expert's testimony will be admissible. In the U.K., courts generally do not admit profiles as evidence. However, the case law on point has been written in such a way that the testimony of profilers may be admissible in the future in the UK.

This means that prosecutors in many jurisdictions can't count on using the testimony of Offender Profilers at court in the prosecution process. It does not mean that the information from the profile itself cannot be used. For example, FBI profilers have been known to coach the investigators to get that information in with their testimony, effectively acting as their own experts in order to overcome admissibility issues at trial. (J. Amber Scherer, 2014).

Introduction to Offender Profiling

Chapter 6 – Other Applications and Conclusions

Other Applications

Previously we discussed ways Offender Profiling can be used to identify a criminal who has already committed a crime. Offender profiling can also be used to determine whether a certain crime is likely or whether a certain person may be likely to commit a crime. Sometimes law enforcement uses Offender Profiling type techniques for these sorts of projects, and sometimes they are even used for other needs.

Law enforcement and/or other such governmental agencies may use Offender Profiling not to catch criminals who have already committed crimes, but to stop crimes before they even happen. For example, law enforcement can do studies of victims of past crimes of a certain type in an area to determine what is causing a certain type of crime to spike in that area. For example, authorities may determine that there has been a pick pocketing spree in certain shopping areas where victims have the tendency to be distracted and apply offender profiling to realize that a certain type of criminal is looking for certain types of victims. Then they can take steps to stop the crimes before they happen, such as by increasing police presence, or by reminding citizens of steps to take to avoid that sort of crime, such as to reminding citizens to watch their purses and wallets when shopping, or by encouraging merchants in areas where the crimes are likely to improve their security systems in ways that the profiler believes are likely to dissuade the criminal from committing the crime in the first place.

Additionally, private entities may use the help of an Offender Profiling in updating their security procedures. For example, a large banking company could hire an offender profiler that could profile bank robbers in the areas where the bank has branches to help the bank determine which branches are more likely to be robbed and therefore need more security devices, or how they need to fix security procedures so they no longer are appealing victims to the people likely to be doing those crimes.

Anyone trained at profiling ultimately can use profiling as a way to predict what others will do based on their profile, and that is something that can be used in a myriad of different ways, from maximizing sales potential of targeted marketing items, to someone determining who may be a good fit as a potential spouse. Because ultimately, Offender Profiling is all about applying psychology to better understand others.

Conclusions

Offender profiling is a new practice that is being used more frequently now than ever before. While it does not live up to the hype from fictional media, it is a practice that is useful to investigators in finding perpetrators in certain types of cases, and also is a practice that has many other possible uses. Because it is a newer field, and because of the limitations on the ability to do scientific experiments, it often is considered more of an art than a science. However, law enforcement agencies are using it more frequently than ever before because they believe it is helping them to solve, and/or prevent, crime.

Bibliography

Bond, Doctor Thomas. 1888. London : s.n., 1888.

Brannen, Keith. 2016. Chart of the Attacks and Murders. *The Yorkshire Ripper.* [Online] April 4, 2016. http://www.execulink.com/~kbrannen/chart.htm.

—. 2016. The Yorkshire Ripper. *The Yorkshire Ripper.* [Online] April 4, 2016. http://www.execulink.com/~kbrannen/.

David V. Canter, Laurence J. Alison, Emily Alison, and Natalia Wentink. 2004. *THE Organized/Disorganized Typology, Myth or Model.* Liverpool : The University of Liverpool, 2004.

Delafuente, Charles. 2004. Terror in the Age of Eisenhower; Recalling the Mad Bomber, Whose Rampage Shook New York. *The New York Times.* September 10, 2004, p. B6.

Doyle, Sir Arthur Conan. 1894. "Adventure 7: The Crooked Man." *The Memoirs of Sherlock Holmes.* Web : Lit2Go Edition, 1894.

Fererro, Gina Limbroso. 1911. *Criminal man, according to the classification of Cesare Lombroso.* New York and London : GP Putnam's Sons, 1911. pp. xiii-xiv.

Goring, Charles. 1913. *The English Convict.* London : His Majesty's Stationary Office, 1913. p. 204.

Guy, Fiona. 2016. Robert Ressler: Pshycgological Profiling of Serial Killers. *Crime Traveller: Crime and the Criminal Mind.* [Online] March 16, 2016. http://www.crimetraveller.org/2016/03/robert-ressler-psychological-profiling/.

Hans Gross, J.U.D. 1918. *Criminal Psychology, a Manual for Judges, Practitioners and Students.* Boston : Little Brown and Company, 1918.

International Academy of Investigative Psychology. 2016. Investigative Psychology: Criminal Actions Create a Shadow... But Psychological Science Can Reveal the Source. *International Academy of Investigative Psychology Website.* [Online] April 4, 2016. http://www.forenspsych.co.uk/Geographical.html.

J. Amber Scherer, M.A., and John P. Jarvis, Ph.D. 2014. Criminal Investigative Analysis: Practitioner Perspectives (Part 1 of 4). *FBI Law Enforcement Bulletin.* June 10, 2014.

John E. Douglas, Robert K. Ressler, Ann W. Burgess, Carol R. Hartman. 1986. *Criminal Profiling from Crime Scene Analysis.* Quantico, Virginia : U.S. Department of Justice, 1986.

King, John Brian. 2000. The Sexual Criminal - The Strange Case of Doctor de River, Part 1. [book auth.] Joseph Paul de River. *The Sexual Criminal.* s.l. : Bloat Books, 2000, pp. xxiii-xxvii.

Langer, Walter. 1943. *Adolf Hitler: Psychological Analysis of Hitler's Life & Legend.* Washington, D.C. : Office of Strategic Services, 1943.

NPR News. 2011. A 16-year Hunt for New York's Mad Bomber. *NPR.* [Online] May 13, 2011. http://www.npr.org/2011/05/13/136287845/a-16-year-hunt-for-new-yorks-mad-bomber.

Parveen, Barbara Davies and Navia. 2015. Why do police want to hide the secrets of little Elsie's savage unsolved murder for 95 years... and is it really linked to the Yorkshire Ripper? . *The Daily Mail.* April 17, 2015.

R H Bull, Charlotte Bilby, Clair Cooke, Tim Hunt, Ruth Hatcher, Jessica Woodhams. 2006. *Criminal Pshychology: A Beginner's Guide.* Oxford : Oneworld Publications, 2006.

Shively, Tom Rich and Michael. 2004. *A Methodology for Evaluating Geographic Profiling Software.* Cambridge, Massachusetts : ABT Associates, Inc., 2004.

Tate, Chris Clark and Tim. 2015. Yorkshire Ripper files reopened: Macabre new clues point to a chilling truth... Peter Sutcliffe butchered not 13 but THIRTY FIVE women and one MAN and, according to a new book, police covered it up. *The Daily Mail.* June 20, 2015.

The Federal Beaureau of Investigation. 2013. Serial Killers Part 2: The Birth of Behavioral Analysis in the FBI. *FBI.* [Online] 10 23, 2013. www.fbi.gov.

The History Channel. 2016. March 29, This Day in History. *History.com.* [Online] March 29, 2016. http://www.history.com/this-day-in-history/the-mad-bomber-strikes-in-new-york.

—. 2016. This Day In History, 1985, the "Railway Rapist" Commits His First Murder. *The History Channel.* [Online] April 5, 2016. http://www.history.com/this-day-in-history/the-railway-rapist-commits-his-first-murder.

The Oxford University Press. 2016. *The Oxford Dictionary of English Online.* London : Oxford University Press, 2016.

Waggoner, Walter H. 1981. Walter Langer Is Dead at 82; Wrote Secret Study of Hitler. *The New York Times.* July 10, 1981.

1936. What is an American? *New York Times.* May 3, 1936, p. 1.

Winerman, Lea. 2004. Criminal Profiling, The Reality Behind the Myth. *American Pshychology Association Monitor on Science.* July/August 2004, p. 66.

Zeigler, Theresa Pinemonti. 2007. Voices--The Albert Dyer Case. *The Daily Mirror.* May 5, 2007, p. 1.

Printed in Great Britain
by Amazon